How to Use Your Snap

This *Academic Writing* Snap Revision Guide will he
written exams. Academic writing isn't as difficult c
means writing like an educated adult.

This guide is divided into three clear sections to help you improve your writing:

Be Concise: your writing shouldn't include unnecessary words or unimportant information. Being concise makes your work read more clearly and, under exam conditions, allows you more time to include the kind of details that will gain marks.

Be Precise: you need to choose words and phrases that convey your exact meaning. Being precise will help you to make your points in a focused, confident and accurate manner.

Be Sophisticated: your style of writing needs to be formal, mature and intelligent. Being sophisticated will mean that your words and sentence structures enhance the meaning that you are trying to convey.

You don't need to include every technique that is explained in this guide in each of your exam answers. By gaining a more secure understanding of academic writing, you will be able to employ the most appropriate techniques depending on the exam question that has been set.

Simply reading this guide will not turn you into an academic writer. You need to refer to it regularly and practise the different techniques; eventually, they will come to you naturally. To help you do this, each section includes the following features:

Examples
Regular modelling of academic writing, based on exams in English Language, English Literature and other GCSE courses such as History, Geography and Science.

Sample paragraphs
Extended examples of the kind of academic writing that you should aim to achieve.

Quick tests and exam practice
Quick-fire tests to check that you have understood the main points from each topic, plus tasks to help you review your previous exam answers in view of the techniques you have explored.

Improve your skills
A series of activities to help you identify and practise successful academic writing.

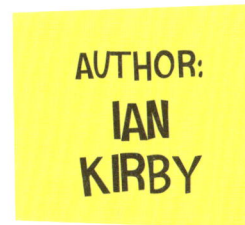

AUTHOR: IAN KIRBY

ebook
To access the ebook version of this Snap Revision Text Guide, visit
collins.co.uk/ebooks
and follow the step-by-step instructions.

Published by Collins
An imprint of HarperCollins*Publishers*
1 London Bridge Street
London SE1 9GF

HarperCollins*Publishers*
1st Floor, Watermarque Building,
Ringsend Road, Dublin 4, Ireland

© HarperCollins*Publishers* Limited 2022

ISBN 978-0-00-852075-5

First published 2022

10 9 8 7 6 5 4 3 2 1

All rights reserved. No part of this publication may be reproduced, stored in a retrieval system, or transmitted in any form or by any means, electronic, mechanical, photocopying, recording or otherwise, without the prior written permission of the Publisher or a licence permitting restricted copying in the United Kingdom issued by the Copyright Licensing Agency Ltd., 90 Tottenham Court Road, London W1T 4LP.

British Library Cataloguing in Publication Data.

A CIP record of this book is available from the British Library.

Commissioning Editor: Claire Souza
Project managers: Fiona Watson and Shelley Teasdale
Author: Ian Kirby
Copy editor: Fiona Watson
Proofreader: Charlotte Christensen
Reviewer: Jo Kemp
Typesetting: Q2A Media
Cover designers: Kneath Associates and Sarah Duxbury
Production: Karen Nulty

Printed in the United Kingdom
by Martins the Printers

ACKNOWLEDGEMENTS
The author and publisher are grateful to the copyright holders for permission to use quoted materials and images.
Every effort has been made to trace copyright holders and obtain their permission for the use of copyright material. The author and publisher will gladly receive information enabling them to rectify any error or omission in subsequent editions. All facts are correct at time of going to press.

MIX
Paper from responsible source
FSC www.fsc.org   FSC™ C007454

This book is produced from independently certified FSC™ paper to ensure responsible forest management.

For more information visit:
www.harpercollins.co.uk/green

Contents

Be Concise
Keep Focused	4
Be Succinct	6
Use Noun Phrases and Nominalisation	8
Improve Your Skills	10

Be Precise
Vocabulary: Best Not Biggest	14
Vocabulary: Subject-Specific Words	16
Establish and Connect Your Ideas	18
Emphasise Understanding and Use Alternative Interpretations	20
Improve Your Skills	22

Be Sophisticated
Be Formal and Use Correct Punctuation	26
Use Variety and Show Caution	28
Use the Third Person and the Passive Voice	30
Integrate and Embed	32
Use Sentence Structures to Enhance Meaning	34
Improve Your Skills	36

In the Exam
Modelled GCSE Answer: English Language	40
Modelled GCSE Answer: English Literature	42
Improve Two GCSE Answers: English Language and English Literature	44

Answers 46

Be Concise › Keep Focused

Read the exam question carefully

Before starting a task, read the question a few times and underline the key words. The most important information to consider is *what* you need to write about and *how*: for example, you might need to describe, explain, analyse, evaluate or compare.

Look at these questions and the key information that has been underlined.

> *Select four facts* about the *weather*.
>
> *How* does Conan Doyle present *Hardcastle's feelings about the weather* in *paragraph 2*?

The first question simply requires four facts about the weather to be extracted from the text. Nothing more. In questions like this, students often give the examiner more than requested.

The second question has a very specific focus: *one character's feelings* about the weather. The word 'how' shows that the answer requires analysis of the author's use of language; a student who simply describes will not get high marks. The question also specifies which part of the text should be analysed; moving beyond this could actually lose marks.

Answer only the question that has been set

Lots of students go to exams with prepared answers in their heads. They end up writing what they know rather than answering the actual questions. Revise thoroughly so you have the knowledge and skills you need to provide correctly focused answers.

Students also tend to write everything they know about a topic or retell the story of the text they have studied. In order to stay focused, make sure you answer *just* the question.

Look at these two answers. Students were asked to explain one cause of the Vietnam War.

> *The 1954 Geneva Accord split Vietnam at the 17th Parallel, creating two ideologically opposed states: the North, led by Ho Chi Minh's communist government, and the South, led by Emperor Bao Dai.*
>
> *The Vietnam War began in 1955, seeing conflict in Vietnam, Laos and Cambodia. There were multiple causes of the war. One of these was the 1954 Geneva Accord which was a result of a conference in Geneva between the US, the USSR, North and South Vietnam and other countries.*

Notice that both answers give a cause for the war but the second contains a lot of unnecessary facts and doesn't explain *why* the stated cause contributed to war.

Summary

- Read the exam question carefully so you know *what* you're writing about and *how* you need to write your answer.
- Don't prepare exam answers. Instead, revise thoroughly and practise exam skills.
- Answer *only* the question – don't try to tell the examiner everything you know.

Be Concise

Sample paragraph

Look at this extract in response to the question: How is the character of Macduff presented in *Macbeth*?

Notice the student's use of specific analysis to respond to the 'how' part of the question, and where extra information has been crossed out to keep the answer focused.

> Macduff is presented as patriotic. ~~He does not appear much in the play but has a central role from the end of Act 4 onwards.~~ The use of personification in his words 'Bleed, bleed, poor country!' shows that he loves Scotland and is pained by how Macbeth's tyranny is affecting his homeland. ~~This is personification because he is describing Scotland as if it is a person.~~ The adjective 'poor' highlights his patriotic sympathy and why he is seeking Malcolm's help to save Scotland. ~~Malcolm's patriotism is also conveyed by Shakespeare's use of personification when he says, 'It weeps, it bleeds', showing his own sorrow for how the country has changed.~~

Questions

QUICK TEST

1. Students were asked to compare how two writers show their feelings about family. What is wrong with the answer below?

    > In Text 1, the writer feels trapped by his family. He describes the baby being 'like a prison of my own making' and the simile shows how he feels he has lost his freedom. The phrase 'my own making' also suggests that he partly blames himself for his situation. In text 2, the writer hates his job and calls it 'misery inducing'. This may be because it is a nightshift so he doesn't get to spend time with his friends.

2. Another question asked students to identify four facts about the house described in a text. To make it more focused, what information should be deleted from the answer below and why?

    > The house has a swimming pool in the basement which is a really relaxing place to swim; the master bedroom is lovely as it has an en suite; the house was originally built in 1888; it is detached which makes it feel quieter and more private.

PRACTISE KEEPING FOCUSED

Look back at one of your previous exam answers from any subject. Can you make it more concise through greater focus?

Keep Focused

Be Concise > Be Succinct

Cut out unnecessary words
Avoid being unnecessarily verbose. Just use the words you need. For example, the following sentence could be more succinct:

The various political policies enacted by the Conservative Party had an undoubtedly significant effect on the economy of the United Kingdom.

Without losing any meaning, it could be reduced to:

Conservative Party policies had a significant effect on the UK's economy.

Resist using unnecessary intensifiers
We often use intensifiers when we speak, in order to convince people that we mean what we say. They are not needed in an essay as they do not demonstrate greater understanding. Look at the unnecessary intensifiers that have been underlined in this sentence.

Sedimentary rock is formed from sediment accumulated over _really_ long periods; it has the highest chance of _definitely_ retaining fossils.

Avoid figurative or descriptive language
When students are struggling to convey an idea, they sometimes resort to adding adjectives or using a simile or metaphor. This is particularly true of students who are creative and well-read. However, an essay should be prosaic rather than poetic. For example, the following sentence uses too much description and figurative language:

Shelley's poem conveys the black hole of loneliness that was engulfing his sad, solitary life.

Plainer language would make the student's idea much more concise:

Shelley's poem conveys his feelings of loneliness.

Beware of repetition
You should avoid repeating ideas across an essay. You should also avoid repeating the same words, or using words that repeat the same meaning, in your sentences. For example, there is no need to include 'repeatedly' as well as 'many' in the following sentence:

Heaney repeatedly explores father–son relationships in many of his poems.

Don't use pairs of synonyms for unnecessary emphasis
Another way students repeat themselves is by using synonym pairs to try to convince the examiner that they understand the topic. However, this does not add any meaning and just takes up time. In the following example, the student only needs one of their synonyms for 'bad':

The effects of the treaty were disastrous and terrible.

Summary

- Don't use unnecessary words.
- Resist unnecessary intensifiers.
- Be prosaic not poetic.
- Avoid repetition and synonym pairs for unnecessary emphasis.

Sample paragraph

Look at the changes that have been made to this paragraph to achieve greater succinctness. Can you see why the changes have been made?

The writer has used the ~~two different~~ adjectives 'dark' and 'isolated'~~, which are describing words,~~ to create a ~~really~~ sinister atmosphere ~~and mood~~, highlighting that the girl is alone ~~and isolated~~ and cannot fully see the contents of the room~~, as if she has been struck blind~~. This is ~~definitely~~ emphasised by the regular use of the onomatopoeia 'tap tap', which suggests there is something ~~going 'tap tap'~~ in the room with the girl ~~and this emphasises the sinister atmosphere~~. Placing the onomatopoeia in short sentences ~~really~~ implies that the girl is aware of the ~~sound of the~~ noise and this is what is most frightening her ~~and filling her with terror~~.

Questions

QUICK TEST

1. What unnecessary words can you spot in this sentence?
    During the scientific process of photosynthesis, plants transform energy from the Sun and this light energy is then converted into chemical energy that the plants need.
2. What unnecessary intensifiers could be removed from this sentence?
    Volcanoes occur when magma rises right to the Earth's surface, creating gas bubbles of really high pressure that eventually explode.
3. How could this sentence be rewritten in a more prosaic style?
    Overcome by waves of guilt, Lady Macbeth begins a dark, spiralling descent into madness.
4. Where does this sentence use unnecessary repetition?
    The poor people and peasants started to revolt in 1381 due to anger and fury at their lack of freedom and equality, and the restrictions placed upon them.

PRACTISE BEING SUCCINCT
Look back at one of your previous exam answers from any subject. Can you make it more concise through greater succinctness?

Be Succinct

Use Noun Phrases and Nominalisation

Be Concise

What is a noun phrase?

A noun phrase is a series of words that combine to describe a thing. Information can be added before and after the noun.

For example, 'car' is a noun, while 'The old car that gathered dust in the garage' is a noun phrase (there are lots of words but the phrase is still about a thing: the car).

Using noun phrases

Noun phrases help with concise writing as they allow us to convey information in a compact way.

You will refer to lots of complicated or multi-faceted *things* in your exams (such as a group of people or places, organisations, a series of chemicals or exercises, geographical features). Try to condense them into noun phrases. You can do this as part of your revision for topics that you know will arise.

For example, 'In 2010, the Government was a coalition that was formed by the Conservative Party and the Liberal Party' could be reduced to the noun phrase 'The Conservative–Liberal coalition government of 2010'.

Nominalisation

Nominalisation is a technique that simply involves turning a verb into a noun (such as 'investigate' becoming 'investigation'), thereby shifting the focus of your answer from actions to concepts. It is particularly useful when you are writing about cause and effect.

For example, changing 'When we explored the reaction of metals to cold water we discovered …' to 'An exploration into the reaction of metals to cold water discovered …' depersonalises the writing and makes the focus more about the concept of a scientific process than the experiment itself.

Similarly, altering 'The Friar decides to secretly marry Romeo and Juliet …' to 'The Friar's decision to secretly marry Romeo and Juliet …' focuses the writing on the key ideas rather than sounding like a retelling of the story.

Nominalisation can also create more concise answers as it often enables you to merge two sentences into one, more sophisticated, sentence. For example, nominalisation could reduce 'Women were traditionally expected to be subservient to men. This makes Lady Macbeth's power over her husband unusual.' to 'Traditional expectations of female subservience make Lady Macbeth's power over her husband unusual.'

Summary

- A noun phrase is a series of words that combine to describe a thing.
- Noun phrases are useful for conveying information in a compact way.
- Nominalisation means turning a verb into a noun.
- Nominalisation helps to focus more on concepts and can create more sophisticated sentences.

Sample paragraph

Notice the use of noun phrases and nominalisation to keep this paragraph concise and focused on the effects of language.

<u>The use of metaphor</u> in the first paragraph conveys <u>her feelings for the baby</u>. <u>Her exclamation</u> 'my heart swells and bursts the first time he smiles' implies that <u>her love for the child</u> is almost overwhelming. <u>The juxtaposition of the complex imagery with the simple verb</u> 'smiles' implies that even a small response from the baby has a big impact on her.

Questions

QUICK TEST
1. Which of these words is a noun? accept, acceptance, acceptable, acceptably
2. Which of these words is a noun? forgiveness, forgivably, forgivable, forgive
3. Turn the underlined section of the following sentence into a noun phrase.
    <u>In 1991, a volcanic eruption occurred on Mount Pinatubo that</u> caused devastation in the Philippines.
4. Use nominalisation to improve the following sentences and combine them into a single sentence.
    The NHS was founded by the Labour Party in 1948. It provided free healthcare for all citizens in the United Kingdom.

PRACTISE USING NOUN PHRASES AND NOMINALISATION
Look back at one of your previous exam answers from any subject. Can you make it more concise and focused through the use of noun phrases and nominalisation?

Use Noun Phrases and Nominalisation

Be Concise — Improve Your Skills

Improve 1

1. Read the two sample paragraphs below. The exam task was to explore the presentation of Mr Hyde in Stevenson's novel *Dr Jekyll and Mr Hyde*. List the ways the second paragraph has been made more concise.

   Stevenson describes Mr Hyde as animalistic with phrases such as 'apelike fury' and 'masked thing like a monkey', drawing on Darwin's theory of evolution, which was published in 1859 in his book 'On the Origin of Species'. Stevenson is also using similes here. It implies that Hyde has devolved, becoming the flipside of the coin in terms of being a Victorian gentleman, and this is massively emphasised by the contrast between 'fury' and the reader's expectations of civilised behaviour. Stevenson shows the reader the expectations of a Victorian gentleman in Chapter 1 when he describes what Mr Utterson is like and how he lives a life of austerity. A sense of disgust and distaste is really conveyed by the noun 'thing', suggesting that Poole (who is telling Utterson what he has seen over the last few evenings) can hardly bring himself to describe Hyde.

   Stevenson's animalistic descriptions of Mr Hyde, such as 'apelike fury' and 'masked thing like a monkey', draw on Darwin's theory of evolution. The implication that Hyde has devolved, becoming the opposite of a Victorian gentleman, is emphasised by the contrast between 'fury' and the reader's expectations of civilised behaviour. A sense of disgust is conveyed by the noun 'thing', suggesting Poole can hardly bring himself to describe Hyde.

2. Read the sample questions below and decide which of the three options best explains what you would need to focus on to produce a concise answer.

   a. Starting with the extract from Act 2 scene 2, how does Shakespeare present Juliet in *Romeo and Juliet*?

      i. Analyse how Shakespeare uses language to show what Juliet is like. Use the extract from Act 2 scene 2 and elsewhere in the play.

      ii. Use the extract from Act 2 scene 2 to analyse how Shakespeare uses language to show what Juliet is like.

      iii. Describe how Juliet behaves in key scenes from *Romeo and Juliet*.

b. How does Ishiguro use the character of Kathy to explore compassion in *Never Let Me Go*?

   i. Analyse how Ishiguro uses language to show what Kathy is like.

   ii. Describe the different points in the novel that show characters being compassionate.

   iii. Focusing on the character of Kathy, analyse how Ishiguro uses language to suggest things about compassion.

c. Find four things about the house in the first paragraph of the text.

   i. Find any four things about the house and write a sentence about each one.

   ii. Analyse how language is used in the text to show what the house is like.

   iii. Using only the first paragraph, list four things about the house.

3. A Geography exam asked for one reason why climate change may cause wider distribution of tropical storms. What aspects have made the answer below unfocused?

   Tropical storms happen around the equator. They are incredibly powerful with wind speeds up to 120km per hour. A rise in temperature due to climate change would create warmer seas, causing the areas where tropical storms form to extend further north and south of the equator. North America and South-East Asia are currently affected by tropical storms which are often referred to as hurricanes, cyclones and typhoons.

Improve 2

4. Rewrite the following paragraph. Remove unnecessary details, unnecessary intensifiers, repetition, pairs of synonyms and figurative language.

   The author begins the story by focusing the reader on the sinister and creepy atmosphere. By describing 'the heavy darkness' and the 'constantly shifting shadows', the author totally unnerves the reader and creates a sense of danger that is like a warning bell for us. This creates an ominous tone which reminds me of an episode of 'Stranger Things'. This ominous tone may be effective in engaging the audience as it grabs the audience's attention and it would make them really consider what will happen when characters and people are introduced to the scene.

5. Rewrite the underlined phrases so they are prosaic rather than figurative.

   a. The political situation at the time was <u>like a bomb waiting to go off</u>.

   b. Many European cities <u>are a melting pot</u> of different cultures.

   c. Lord Capulet <u>sees red</u> when Juliet refuses to marry Paris.

   d. Social media use has <u>exploded</u> in the 21st century.

   e. Macbeth <u>starts to behave like a monster</u>.

6. Shorten the underlined sections by turning them into noun phrases.
   a. <u>Priestley's play was written in the 1940s and</u> is a classic work of 20th-century drama.
   b. <u>The experiment was about seeds and</u> explored the process of germination.
   c. <u>In Java, there are lots of volcanoes that are active and they</u> continue to be monitored by the authorities.

Improve 3

7. Copy the following table and change the verbs to nouns (using suffixes like -tion, -y and -ment).

Verb	Noun	Verb	Noun
Concludes		Interprets	
Creates		Introduces	
Decides		Produces	
Develops		Succeeds	
Explores		Summarises	

8. Rephrase the sentences below to change the underlined verbs into nouns.
   a. I can <u>conclude</u> that plants need light to survive.
   b. Benvolio is <u>developed</u> by Shakespeare to display a more serious side of the character.
   c. When he <u>introduces</u> Jack, Golding adds tension to chapter 1.

9. Use nominalisation to improve the following sentences.
   a. Sheila is feeling remorse at the end of the play and this leads her into conflict with her parents.
   b. In 1916, the government introduced the Military Service Act which imposed conscription on all single men between 18 and 41. This then provided the United Kingdom with the soldiers it needed to continue fighting the war.

Be Concise

Improve 4

10. Read the following extract from an essay about the presentation of Lord Capulet in *Romeo and Juliet*. Think about where the paragraph could be more concise then rewrite it.

    Consider:

    - focus
    - unnecessary words
    - unnecessary intensifiers
    - figurative or descriptive language
    - repetition
    - synonym pairs
    - noun phrases and nominalisation.

    > In Act 3 scene 5, Lord Capulet is presented as authoritarian and cruel when he gives Juliet the ultimatum to marry Paris or 'hang! Beg! Starve! Die in the streets! / For by my soul I'll ne'er acknowledge thee'. This is very very different from the loving father of Act 1 scene 2 who treated Juliet as if she were the apple of his eye. Shakespeare can be seen using a list of verbs, which are doing words, to convey Capulet's cruelty and harshness but also his awareness of the economic power he has over his daughter: she has been totally brought up to rely on a father or husband, rather than to have the ability to support herself or become economically independent. Lady Capulet has also created this role for Juliet by continually romanticising marriage, for example in Act 1 scene 3, and presenting it as Juliet's only option. The exclamation marks suggest the words should be shouted, increasing the audience's sense of his power. This shouting will make him seem dominant and in control. When Capulet makes a threat to cut Juliet off from the family it emphasises and highlights his harshness, revealing that his previous unconditional love for her is dependent upon her following his orders and rules.

Be Precise > Vocabulary: Best Not Biggest

Focus on meaning

Too often, students try to impress by using lots of big words. However, this can actually detract from the meaning you are trying to convey.

Make sure that you choose the words that have the closest meaning to what you want to say.

For example, stating that the character of Sheila from the play *An Inspector Calls* is 'self-satisfied' is precise. Two words with *similar* meanings to 'satisfied' are 'fulfilled' and 'satiated'; however, they don't have the *same* meaning. If you described Sheila as 'self-fulfilled' or 'self-satiated', your comments would not be accurate.

Improve the precision of your vocabulary

Whenever you are considering using a big word, take the time to check its meaning in a dictionary. If its definition isn't quite what you are aiming for, find a different word.

A thesaurus is an excellent resource for finding new words but the synonyms provided have similar meanings, rather than being exactly the same. Again, it is important to check individual definitions in a dictionary.

If you come across an unusual word when you are reading, don't just guess its meaning. Check it and then try to use it in your own writing.

Show shades of meaning

It is good to learn synonyms in terms of scales of intensity. This will allow you to use them more precisely and will also help you to convey how something alters or builds up.

For example, contented, cheerful, overjoyed and ecstatic are all synonyms for happy. However, notice that those four words convey different degrees of happiness. Saying someone felt cheerful when they won ten million pounds might be understating their reaction, while describing someone as ecstatic upon being bought an ice cream would probably be an overstatement.

Think about your exam topics and consider whether you will need to show shades of meaning. For instance, if you are studying a horror story, it would be good to learn a range of words that show different degrees of fear.

Summary

- The biggest word is not necessarily the best. Focus on precision of meaning.
- Use a thesaurus and a dictionary to gradually build up a precise vocabulary.
- Be aware that synonyms can show different degrees of meaning.
- Think about your exam topics and learn vocabulary banks that display shades of meaning.

Sample paragraph

The following paragraph is from an essay on the novel *Never Let Me Go*. The language used is precise. Look at the underlined words and consider why the synonyms given below would have been imprecise.

Kathy's sympathy[1] for Tommy is established by Ishiguro at the start of the novel. Seeing Tommy's embarrassment[2] she describes 'a little stab of pain' and this metaphor shows that his treatment caused her some discomfort[3]. However, the use of the adjective 'little' implies that her feelings for Tommy were less strong[4] at the time and she wasn't overly concerned by how he was bullied[5].

1. Congeniality
2. Unease
3. Soreness
4. Athletic
5. Terrorised

Questions

QUICK TEST
Select the most precise synonym in each sentence. Use a dictionary if it helps.
1. Romeo and Juliet **admire / love / venerate** each other.
2. At the start of the play, Macbeth is presented as **law-abiding / chivalrous / honourable**.
3. It is **bad / lousy / shocking** when Mr Hyde stamps upon the child's body.
4. In *The Merchant of Venice*, Shylock is presented as **hungry / avaricious / tight**.

PRACTISE USING THE BEST VOCABULARY
Look back at one of your previous exam answers from any subject. Can you improve the precision of your vocabulary?

Vocabulary: Subject-Specific Words

Be Precise

Subject-specific words

It is important that you know, understand and can spell the key terminology that appears in each of your exam subjects.

Whether you have exams in English, History, Geography, Drama, Physics, Biology or Chemistry, there will be subject-specific language that you should be using regularly.

For example, in English Literature, you will need to know words like verb, noun, adjective, adverb, metaphor, simile, personification, symbolise, repetition, quotation, character, imply, convey, emphasise, alternatively and comparison.

Correctly using terminology like this shows that you have a full academic understanding of the subject.

Make a list of key words for each of your subjects. Cross off the terms you are confident about and focus on any you have not yet secured.

Topic-specific words

As well as broad subject-specific words, you should also learn any key terminology that features in the individual topics you have studied. This will help to show that you have an in-depth understanding of the topic.

For example, if you are studying *Macbeth*, you would benefit from knowing words like allegiance, ambition, conscience, corruption, damnation, emasculate, equivocal, honour, manipulate, redemption, regicide, sanity and tyranny.

It is worth considering how the endings of your key words can be altered so they can be used in different contexts, such as manipulate / manipulated / manipulating / manipulation / manipulative / manipulator.

Your lists should also include important proper nouns such as the names of authors, inventors, characters, historical figures and countries.

Practise using key words

It isn't enough simply to know your subject- and topic-specific words. You need to be able to apply them in a written exam.

Practise using them in sentences so you know how to include them in an essay. For example:

> Macbeth initially shows <u>allegiance</u> to the King. However, his <u>ambitions</u> eventually overrule his <u>conscience</u> and the audience witness his increasing <u>corruption</u>.

If you're not sure that a phrase sounds precise when you use it, check the words in a dictionary or ask the advice of a teacher, friend or relative.

Summary

- Make sure you know, understand and can spell the key terminology for each of your exam subjects.
- Develop your vocabulary further with topic-specific words.
- Practise using your subject-specific vocabulary so you can apply it effectively in examinations.

Sample paragraph

Look at this extract from an essay about the play *An Inspector Calls*. Notice the subject-specific and topic-specific language.

Priestley's exploration of the theme of social responsibility is conveyed through the lines he gives to the Inspector about society. When he announces, 'We don't live alone. We are members of one body. We are responsible for each other', the plural pronoun 'we' is repeated in a pattern of three statements to emphasise the socialist value of joint responsibility. The short sentences emphasise the message that we should all respect and help each other and this is highlighted by the metaphor 'one body'.

Questions

QUICK TEST
1. What is the difference between subject-specific and topic-specific words?
2. Which of these is the correct spelling?

    a. similey   simile   similie
    b. metaphor   metaphore   metafore
    c. cymbalism   symbalism   symbolism
    d. repetition   repitition   repatition
    e. charachter   charactor   character

PRACTISE USING SUBJECT-SPECIFIC VOCABULARY
Look back at one of your previous exam answers from any subject. Underline all the subject-specific and topic-specific words you have used. Could you have included more to improve your level of precision?

Vocabulary: Subject-Specific Words

Establish and Connect Your Ideas

Be Precise

Use topic sentences

To increase the precision of your writing, you should use different techniques to help the examiner keep track of your answer. This is particularly important in longer essays.

One way to achieve this is to include topic phrases or sentences at the start of your paragraphs or points in order to establish the focus.

Look at these examples:

Andrew Johnson's effectiveness as president has divided historians …

The main social opportunities created by urban growth are access to services and resources …

Once you have established the focus of your point or paragraph, it is important to maintain it and develop your ideas appropriately. When you are ready to move on to another idea, signal this to the examiner by starting a new paragraph and writing a new topic sentence.

Use demonstrative links

When developing your ideas, try to link them together. This proves that you have a precise understanding of the question and are not simply telling the examiner everything you know, whether it is relevant or not.

One way to create links between your sentences is by using the four demonstratives: this, that, these, those. For example:

This absorption of energy by atoms causes …

These old-fashioned attitudes towards gender are apparent in …

Demonstratives highlight that you are taking a key point from your previous sentence and developing it further.

Use development links

It is also important to create links between your paragraphs as this helps to make a whole essay cohesive.

This can be achieved by using discourse markers (or connective phrases) at the start of your topic sentences. You should select these precisely, according to the type of essay you have been asked to write.

You will often need phrases that show you are building up an idea, such as 'in addition', 'furthermore', 'as well as this' and 'moreover'.

In a comparative essay, you should also employ phrases like 'similarly', 'in comparison', 'however', 'in contrast' and 'conversely'.

An essay that needs to convey sequences as well as cause and effect might include phrases such as 'firstly', 'next', 'subsequently', 'finally', 'consequently', 'because', 'due to' and 'as a result'.

Many of these words and phrases can also be useful within your paragraphs to link your sentences together.

Summary

- Use topic sentences or phrases at the start of paragraphs to establish your focus.
- Use demonstratives to link the sentences within your paragraphs.
- Use discourse markers to link sentences and paragraphs.

Sample paragraph

This is an extract from an English Language exam, analysing how a setting has been presented. Notice the different techniques used by the student to help the examiner keep track of their answer.

The writer presents the house as old and neglected. This can be seen in the opening description of its 'cracked windows and cobwebbed walls', where the adjectives suggest a lack of repair and cleanliness. These images are enhanced by the simile 'like an abandoned car', which implies that no-one has paid any attention to the building for a long time. Furthermore, the repeated references to 'dust' and 'dirt' highlight these impressions that the house is uncared for.

In addition, the house is given a sense of mystery …

Questions

QUICK TEST
1. What are the four demonstratives?
2. Do the following discourse markers suggest addition, cause and effect, sequence or comparison/contrast?
    a. Thirdly …
    b. Moreover …
    c. Whereas …
    d. On account of this …
    e. Equally …

PRACTISE ESTABLISHING AND CONNECTING YOUR IDEAS
Look back at one of your previous exam answers from any subject. Can you improve your use of topic sentences, demonstrative links and development links?

Establish and Connect Your Ideas

Be Precise: Emphasise Understanding and Use Alternative Interpretations

Elaboration

To show a precise understanding of the topic you are being examined on, it is good to elaborate upon the points that you make.

One effective way to do this is to use a colon to introduce your elaboration. For example, when writing about the character of Mr Birling in the play *An Inspector Calls*, you might make the point that 'Mr Birling is portrayed as a selfish businessman'.

However, you could show a more precise understanding of the character by elaborating on your statement. Look at the how the colon has been used to introduce the elaboration in the sentence below.

> Mr Birling is portrayed as a selfish businessman: he values profit over principles, shows little care for the welfare of his workers, and even sees his daughter's marriage as a way to improve his business.

Each of these ideas could then be evidenced and analysed, creating a more in-depth exploration of the character.

Whenever you use a colon, make sure that the clause that precedes it makes complete sense on its own.

Restating

Another way to emphasise your understanding is to restate your main points, using phrases like 'In other words' or 'In essence'. For example, a student of Physical Education might write:

> During exercise, inhalation becomes more frequent because the muscles have a greater need for oxygen and energy. In other words, aerobic activity will cause breathing to be quicker and heavier.

The student isn't simply repeating their answer. The first sentence explains how breathing changes during exercise and why; the second sentence then restates the essential point about how aerobic exercise affects breathing.

Alternative interpretation

In some exam subjects, you can also show precision and range of understanding by including alternatives. This shows the examiner that you have a clear viewpoint but are also aware of other perspectives.

For example, if writing about Wordsworth's 'The Prelude', you might analyse how the narrator's feelings of strength and power are presented by describing the 'little' boat and the way in which he uses his 'skill' to manoeuvre it in an 'unswerving line'. You might then add a sentence that shows an alternative reading. For example:

> However, the adjective 'little' could also be used to foreshadow his feelings of insignificance once he is left in awe by the power of the natural world.

Summary

- Emphasise your understanding by using a colon to elaborate upon an idea.
- Emphasise your understanding by using a phrase like 'In other words …' to restate an idea.
- Where relevant, emphasise your precision and range of understanding by acknowledging alternative perspectives.

Sample paragraph

Notice the use of elaboration, restating and alternatives in this extract from an essay exploring the character of Sheila from *An Inspector Calls*.

By Act 2, Priestley presents Sheila as reflecting on her actions: <u>she displays guilt, regret and an understanding of personal responsibility</u>. Telling the Inspector, 'I know I'm to blame – and I'm desperately sorry', the use of the adverb 'desperately' highlights her sense of wrongdoing while the pause indicates she is considering what she has done. This is also shown by the repetition of 'I'm' to reinforce the idea of individual culpability; <u>in other words</u>, she accepts her part in Eva Smith's fate. <u>However</u>, when she adds 'but I can't believe – I won't believe – it's simply my fault', this acceptance is juxtaposed with a refusal to take ultimate responsibility. <u>In essence</u>, she is hoping that her own guilt will be assuaged by that of the other characters.

Questions

QUICK TEST
1. When using a colon, what must you always ensure about the clause that precedes it?
2. Where would the colon be placed in the following sentence of elaboration?
    Climate change will affect our world in multiple ways environmentally, economically and socially.
3. What phrases can you use to restate an idea?
4. Why can it be good to include alternative perspectives?

PRACTISE EMPHASISING UNDERSTANDING AND USING ALTERNATIVE INTERPRETATIONS
Look back at one of your previous exam answers from any subject. Can you increase your precision by using elaboration or restating to show your understanding? Are there any opportunities for exploring alternative perspectives?

Emphasise Understanding and Use Alternative Interpretations

Be Precise > Improve Your Skills

Improve 1

1. Read the two sample paragraphs below. The exam task was to explore how Lady Macbeth is presented as changing in Shakespeare's play *Macbeth*; this is an extract from towards the end of the essay. List what has been done to make the second paragraph more precise.

   In Act 5 scene 1, Shakespeare gives Lady Macbeth the lines, 'Out, damned spot! out, I say! – One: two: why, then, 'tis time to do't. – Hell is murky!' These lines show that she is stricken by madness and she shows none of her previous skills of speech. The way it has been written indicates that her speech should be performed in a way that sounds completely insane. The references to the murder of the King (the 'spot' of blood and 'time to do't') suggest that her madness has been caused by the fact that she feels bad for her part in the killing of the King.

   Whereas she is calm and manipulative earlier in the play, by Act 5 scene 1 Lady Macbeth is presented as being stricken by madness. This is conveyed through deliberately disconnected sentences such as, 'Out, damned spot! out, I say! – One: two: why, then, 'tis time to do't. – Hell is murky!', which show none of her previous skills of rhetoric: she now seems barely coherent. The regular pauses and exclamation marks indicate that her speech should be performed in a distracted yet urgent tone. In other words, she appears out of control rather than controlling. The references to the murder of the King (the 'spot' of blood and 'time to do't') suggest that this madness has been caused by her guilt, contrasting with her unconcerned attitude in Act 2 scene 2. Alternatively, as regicide was seen as a crime against God, the adjective 'damned' and the comment that 'Hell is murky' could imply that it is a fear of eternal punishment that has caused this insanity.

2. Read the sentences of poetry analysis below and replace 'words' or 'phrase' with precise subject-specific language.
   a. At the start of the poem, Waterhouse uses the <u>words</u> 'scramble … pushing … trying' to convey his determination to form a clear memory of his grandfather.
   b. The <u>words</u> 'young' and 'frightened' create sympathy for the bride as they depict her innocence and how she should not have been married off to the farmer.
   c. Wordsworth's <u>phrase</u> 'heaving through the water like a swan' conveys the satisfaction he takes from his ability to control the boat's movement across the lake.
   d. The <u>phrase</u> 'I am branded by an impression of sunlight' is used by Rumens to suggest that, despite the trauma of having to leave, the speaker cannot forget that her homeland was once a happy place.
   e. Owen uses the <u>phrase</u> 'Dawn massing in the east her melancholy army' to suggest that the real threat to the soldiers is the harsh weather conditions.

3. a. Choose a subject that you are studying where you think you need to improve your use of vocabulary. Create a table like the one below. In the left-hand column, make a list of broad terminology that you use regularly within that subject. For the right-hand column, select an individual topic or unit from that subject and make a list of topic-specific words. Ensure that all of your words are spelled correctly. Use your revision notes to help you complete this task.

Subject:	Topic:

   You should repeat this task for any subjects or topics where your vocabulary needs improving.

   b. Focus on the subject-specific and topic-specific words with which you aren't yet comfortable. Try to write a paragraph, making accurate use of as many of those words as you can.

Improve 2

4. Read the sentences below and choose a more precise alternative for each word or phrase that has been underlined.
   a. Climate change is a <u>formidable</u> issue.
   b. Too much screen-time can <u>mutilate</u> people's eyes.
   c. The reviewer <u>luxuriated</u> in the book and awarded it 3 out of 5.
   d. The girl was <u>enervated</u> after the 5000-metre run.

5. Thinking about shades of meaning, reorganise these lists of words to show increasing intensity.

   a. Delighted   Jubilant   Merry   Pleased   Satisfied

   b. Miserable   Downcast   Sorry   Heartbroken   Unhappy

   c. Deadly   Risky   Threatening   Treacherous   Uncertain

6. a. Again, thinking about shades of meaning, reorganise these words to show increasing intensity.

   Creepy   Frightening   Sinister   Strange   Terrifying

   b. What other synonyms can you think of for 'scary'? Do you think they have low, average or high intensity?

   c. Using some of the words from tasks a and b above, write a paragraph analysing how the text below is made increasingly frightening by the author.

   > The wind brushed through the trees like a whisper as the full moon shone on the graveyard. Amidst the swirls of dense fog, shadows flitted between the tombstones. Suddenly, a scream ripped through the night: a blood-curdling cry of shock and pain.

   d. Choose an adjective that you think you are likely to need synonyms for in one of your exams (for example 'funny' or 'cruel'). Make a list of alternatives, arranged on a scale of intensity.

Improve 3

7. Read the short paragraph below. Then decide which of the three topic sentences would be most effective to begin the paragraph.

   > Arthur tells Eric and Gerald that 'a man has to mind his own business', using a double meaning to suggest both the importance of making money and the idea of ignoring the plight of others. This is emphasised when he uses the phrase 'look after himself and his own' to promote selfishness and imply that poorer people are somehow beneath him and need to help themselves.

   a. Arthur displays firm beliefs in Act 1 of *An Inspector Calls*.

   b. In *An Inspector Calls*, Arthur displays a firm belief in the survival of the fittest.

   c. In *An Inspector Calls*, Priestley includes a conversation between Arthur, Gerald and Eric which tells us important ideas about the play.

Be Precise

8. a. Develop the following sentences by using a colon to add elaborative information.
    - Shakespeare's plays can be sorted into three different genres.
    - The periodic table is structured to show periodic trends of the chemical elements.
   b. Develop this answer by restating the main idea.

   Photosynthesis is the process by which green plants use the energy of light to convert carbon dioxide and water into sugar glucose, consequently releasing oxygen into the atmosphere. In other words, plants …

9. The paragraph below compares how war is presented in the poems 'Exposure' (by Wilfred Owen) and 'The Charge of the Light Brigade' (by Alfred Tennyson). Use topic sentences, demonstrative links and development links to improve the student's answer.

   Owen focuses on the brutal conditions: 'the merciless iced east winds that knive us', using personification to suggest that the men feel under attack by the weather. A sense of attack is highlighted by the use of the verb 'knive' to convey the soldiers' physical pain, and the way the adjective 'merciless' suggests there is no respite. Tennyson focuses on the fighting. His use of anaphora in 'Cannon to right of them, / Cannon to left of them, / Cannon behind them' creates an image of soldiers being under constant attack. The use of the prepositions emphasises that there is no escape.

Be Formal and Use Correct Punctuation

Formality

The most important aspect of academic writing is not writing how you speak or text. We vary our formality according to the situation we are in. For example:

Increasing formality

Examples of speech	Examples of writing
Relaxing with friends	Texting friends
Contributing in class	Texting family
Meeting the headteacher	Making notes on a topic
Being interviewed for a job	Emailing a teacher
Making an official presentation	Writing an essay

Your essays need to read more like a school textbook or an article in a broadsheet newspaper, rather than resembling a chat with friends.

Some ways to be more formal:

- Avoid chatty phrases such as 'like' or 'you know' and slang such as 'gonna' or 'kids'.
- Avoid incomplete sentences: each one should make sense if read in isolation.
- Reduce the number of contractions you use ('can't' / 'cannot').
- Use formal grammar, especially for plurals, such as 'he is' / 'they are'.
- Do not address the examiner (e.g. 'You might think that Macbeth is all bad but you'd be wrong.') or pose rhetorical questions (e.g. 'Homeostasis is the body's capacity to maintain steady physical and chemical conditions. But how is that achieved?').
- Avoid unnecessary exclamation marks and multiple forms of punctuation (e.g. 'The opening sentence of the story is very unusual!! What is the main character doing?!').

Correct punctuation

A higher level of formality can also be achieved through correct punctuation. Make regular use of a full stop followed by a capital letter. If you are using a second conjunction in your sentence, like 'and' or 'but', it is often a good idea to change that conjunction into a full stop and start a new sentence.

Use apostrophes correctly for abbreviation or ownership.

Use commas in lists and also to separate clauses. Most sentences should contain a main clause (which makes sense on its own) and a subordinate clause (which does not make sense on its own). For example, 'Set in the late 1960s, *Anita and Me* explores attitudes to race in the fictional Midlands town of Tollington.' If you find that the clauses on both sides of your comma make sense on their own, alter one of the clauses or simply change the comma to a conjunction or a full stop.

Summary

- Increase your level of formality when writing your exam answers.
- Avoid features of everyday speech and texting such as slang, chattiness, incorrect grammar and multiple forms of punctuation.
- Aim for correct punctuation by securing your use of full stops, clauses and commas.

Sample paragraph

Identify as many differences as you can between an informal text and a piece of academic writing. Start by noticing the length or complexity of the words and sentence structures.

Can u guys decide lol
Either town or jacks house
Tell me where ur goin so I can find ya!!

In Duffy's poem, the man photographs a dead body in a way that would normally seem inappropriate. The lines 'he sought approval / without words to do what someone must' use a modal verb to imply that he feels he has no choice because of the situation he is in. Although he specifies that he gets permission, it is clear he places documenting a war above more usual emotions and reactions to death.

Questions

QUICK TEST
1. Where should the comma be placed in this sentence?
    Reigning from 1558 to 1603 one of Elizabeth I's main priorities was England's national security.
2. Where should the comma be placed in this sentence?
    Despite threats from Catholics and Puritans Elizabeth changed the country's official religion to Protestantism.
3. Where should the comma be placed in this sentence?
    Often called the 'golden age' of culture Elizabeth's reign saw theatre becoming popular throughout society.
4. What is wrong with this sentence and how could it be corrected?
    Tensions grew between Spain and England, this culminated in an attack by the Spanish Armada in 1588.

PRACTISE BEING FORMAL AND USING CORRECT PUNCTUATION
Look back at one of your previous exam answers from any subject. Can you improve its level of formality and its use of punctuation?

Be Sophisticated: Use Variety and Show Caution

Vary your vocabulary

Academic writing becomes more sophisticated if a variety of vocabulary is used to give it flair and make it more engaging. Repetitive language can be boring and imply a lack of effort, so avoid using the same term several times. For example, if you are writing about 'crime', you might use alternatives like 'misdemeanour', 'felony' or 'wrongdoing'. However, remember to maintain your precision by ensuring that the meanings of your words match what you want to say.

Vary your sentence openers

Make sure you are not always using the same first word or phrase at the start of sentences. Students often repeat words like 'The' or 'It' and phrases like 'In the text' or 'The author suggests'. This doesn't make the answer wrong but it does make it less sophisticated.

Similarly, use a variety of development links or connective phrases. An essay that keeps repeating 'Also …' or that opens paragraphs with 'Firstly … Secondly … Finally …' will not sound as academic as it could.

Vary your sentence structures

Sophistication can also be achieved by varying the way you construct your sentences. Once you have secured your use of a comma to separate the main clause and subordinate clause in a complex sentence, you can start to vary where you place your subordinate clauses. They can go before, after or in the middle of your main clauses. For example:

- Asserting that she is not attractive enough, Mr Darcy does not dance with Elizabeth.
- Mr Darcy does not dance with Elizabeth, asserting that she is not attractive enough.
- Mr Darcy, asserting that she is not attractive enough, does not dance with Elizabeth. (Notice there are commas either side of the subordinate clause.)

Use cautious language

Sometimes you will be exploring an issue rather than providing a definitive answer. For example, the English Language exam will expect you to explore different perspectives. You can bring sophistication to your writing by using cautious language that allows for other possibilities, outcomes or interpretations (e.g. appears, suggests, indicates, implies; may, might, could, perhaps).

Your sentence structures can also be used to express caution. For example, you could present one possible idea in the subordinate clause and follow it up with your preferred idea in the main clause:

> *Although it could be claimed that …, it may also be asserted …*
>
> *While it can be observed that …, there is evidence to suggest …*

Summary

- Avoid repeating the same words in your answer.
- Vary your sentence openers and development links.
- Move the position of the subordinate clause in complex sentences to keep them varied.
- Show caution through your language and sentence structures.

Sample paragraph

This sample paragraph is part of an essay exploring how the character of Mr Hyde is presented as violent. Notice how the student has varied their language and sentence structures, and shown some caution in their interpretation.

> Mr Hyde's brutality is perhaps most apparent in his killing of Carew. Stevenson introduces the murder as being an act of 'ferocity', highlighting this aspect of Hyde's character by juxtaposing his behaviour with that of his victim. Whereas Carew is described as 'a beautiful gentleman … with a very pretty manner of politeness', Hyde 'broke out in a great flame of anger … like a madman'. As well as the contrast between 'gentleman' and 'madman', the metaphor for Hyde's sudden rage conveys his viciousness compared to Carew's 'politeness'.

Questions

QUICK TEST

1. Considering the words that have been underlined, rewrite the two sentences below with more varied vocabulary.

   > The first paragraph shows how cold the boy is, with verbs like 'shivering' showing his reaction to the cold. The setting also shows this by its use of nouns like 'icicle' and 'snow' to show that it is cold.

2. How could you bring caution to the way the sentence below has been written?

   > When Heaney describes his father and the horse as a 'sweating team … his eye narrowed and angled at the ground', it means that he was impressed by how hard his father worked.

PRACTISE USING VARIETY AND CAUTION

Look back at one of your previous exam answers from any subject. Can you bring greater sophistication to your writing by improving the variety of your vocabulary and sentence structures? Can you also find any opportunities to use caution within your answer?

Use Variety and Show Caution

Use the Third Person and the Passive Voice

Be Sophisticated

Avoid using 'I'

Academic writing is objective. It focuses on ideas and concepts that are supported by evidence rather than personal opinions. Unless you are specifically asked for your view, remove words like 'I' and 'my' from your writing and use the third person.

Also avoid using first-person filler phrases such as 'personally', 'for me' and 'in my opinion'. The examiner knows you are the writer so you don't need to keep pointing it out.

Using the third rather than the first person also makes your writing sound more confident. This table shows how you might change some first-person comments into the third person.

First person	Third person
I think this poem is about …	This poem explores …
I found that …	It was discovered that …
My investigation showed …	The investigation showed …
In my opinion …	It could be argued that …

What are active and passive voice?

Writing has an active or a passive voice.

In the active voice, the subject of a sentence does something to the object. For example, 'Pebbles and stones wear away the riverbank and bed.' In this sentence, the subject is 'pebbles and stones' and the object is 'the riverbank and bed'.

In the passive voice, the subject does not do something – it has something done to it. For example, 'The riverbank and bed are worn away by pebbles and stones.' In this version, the subject is 'the riverbank and bed' and it has something done to it by the object, 'pebbles and stones'.

When to use the passive voice

It often feels more natural to write in the active voice and this style can be useful for clarifying key events, important people or characters, authorial intent, etc. However, the passive voice is often preferable in academic writing – especially for scientific subjects – because it helps to focus your work on the results of actions rather than who or what is doing those actions. The passive voice will make your writing sound more conceptual rather than descriptive.

In the previous examples, the passive voice strengthened the focus on the geographical effects of abrasion. Similarly, the sentence 'The benefits of trade expansion were recognised by Elizabeth I.' sounds more focused on a historical issue than 'Elizabeth I recognised the benefits of trade expansion.'

Be Sophisticated

Summary

- Use the third person to sound objective rather than personal.
- In the active voice, the subject of a sentence does something to the object.
- The active voice can be useful for clarifying key events or roles.
- In the passive voice, the subject of the sentence has something done to it by the object.
- The passive voice is important in academic writing to increase your focus on consequences and concepts.

Sample paragraph

Notice how the lack of a first-person perspective keeps the tone of this paragraph objective and scientific rather than personal. The use of the passive voice keeps the focus on the topic of the key substances and what happens to them (instead of the focus being on the blood).

> Key substances are transported in the body's blood. Oxygen is carried from the lungs to all the cells of the body by blood, while carbon dioxide is carried from the cells of the body to the lungs. In addition, glucose is transferred from the digestive system to the liver and then to the body's cells by the same means.

Questions

QUICK TEST
1. Is the first person personal or objective?
2. Rewrite this sentence in the third person.
    I think Shakespeare presents Macbeth as a tragically flawed individual.
3. What is the difference between the active and passive voice?
4. Rewrite this sentence in the passive voice.
    Priestley presents Mrs Birling as a hypocrite.

PRACTISE USING THE THIRD PERSON AND PASSIVE VOICE
Look back at one of your previous exam answers, especially from your science subjects. Can you improve the sophistication of your response by using the third person and the passive voice?

Be Sophisticated: Integrate and Embed

Blend different aspects of your answer

To achieve full marks for your exam answers you need to include a range of different information. For example, for the Shakespeare task in English Literature, you need to show a clear understanding of how the play relates to the exam question, select quotations, analyse Shakespeare's use of language, and link your comments to the play's context.

You could accomplish this by including four different sentences in each of your paragraphs: point, evidence, analysis and context. However, it is more sophisticated to integrate and embed these different aspects of your answer into two or three sentences.

Embed your evidence

A key skill that you should try to master is embedding evidence. Students often tag it onto the end of a sentence or isolate it in a separate sentence. For example: 'Shakespeare presents Tybalt as aggressive and arrogant during his argument with Lord Capulet in Act 1 scene 5: "I'll not endure him."' It is much better to merge it into the sentence: 'Shakespeare presents Tybalt as aggressive and arrogant when he asserts "I'll not endure him" during his argument with Lord Capulet in Act 1 scene 5.'

Develop your integration

Once you can embed your evidence, think about other aspects of your answer that can be integrated to create a more sophisticated response.

Look at the paragraph below about how Shakespeare has presented the character of Juliet. Notice that there is a clear point, well-selected evidence, accurate use of terminology, insightful analysis and a relevant link to the play's context.

> Shakespeare presents Juliet as cautious in Act 2 scene 2. 'It is too rash, too unadvised, too sudden.' There is a pattern of three. Shakespeare shows that Juliet is worried that the relationship is advancing too quickly and that her behaviour is imprudent. This is emphasised by the repetition of 'too'. Her caution could link to how young ladies of wealthy families would be brought up to behave in a restrained and respectable manner.

Now look at the improved paragraph below. It contains the same information but in an integrated manner. The evidence and terminology have been integrated with part of the analysis; the context has been relocated so it is no longer tagged on the end, instead being used to lead into the other part of the analysis.

> Shakespeare presents Juliet as cautious. In Act 2 scene 2, the pattern of three 'It is too rash, too unadvised, too sudden' emphasises her fears that the relationship is advancing too quickly. This could link to how young ladies of wealthy families would be brought up to behave in a restrained and respectable manner, which is highlighted by her repetition of 'too' to suggest she considers her behaviour to be imprudent.

Remember your punctuation

When integrating, you must not simply turn your full stops into commas and let your sentences run on. Make sure your work is still grammatically correct.

Summary

- Embed your evidence.
- Integrate information to create a more cohesive response.
- Make sure that you maintain accurate punctuation.

Sample paragraph

Look at these three versions of a paragraph about guilt in Shakespeare's play *Macbeth*. The first is good but not integrated; the second is partially integrated but incorrectly punctuated; the third is integrated, accurate and sophisticated.

> Macbeth feels guilty after the murder. 'Will all great Neptune's ocean wash this blood / Clean from my hand?' Shakespeare uses hyperbole. This conveys the depth of Macbeth's guilt. There is also a rhetorical question. This emphasises the anxiety that his guilt is causing him.

> Macbeth's guilt after the murder is shown in the rhetorical question, 'Will all great Neptune's ocean wash this blood / Clean from my hand?', Shakespeare uses hyperbole, conveying the depth of his feelings, and structures the lines in the form of a question, emphasising the anxiety that this guilt is causing Macbeth.

> Macbeth's guilt after the murder is conveyed in the rhetorical question, 'Will all great Neptune's ocean wash this blood / Clean from my hand?', where Shakespeare uses hyperbole to convey the depth of his feelings. Structuring the lines in the form of a question also emphasises the anxiety that this remorse is causing Macbeth.

Questions

QUICK TEST

Rewrite these sentences so that the evidence or examples are embedded.
1. The Battle of Stamford Bridge was a decisive victory for King Harold. It ended in the killing of Godwinson, Hardrada and the majority of the Norwegian forces.
2. Various strategies can be used to reduce the risk of desertification. Water and soil management, tree planting and use of appropriate technology.

PRACTISE EMBEDDING AND INTEGRATION

Look back at one of your previous exam answers, especially from English Literature. Can you improve the sophistication of your response by embedding your evidence and integrating your ideas?

Integrate and Embed

Use Sentence Structures to Enhance Meaning

Be Sophisticated

Establish ideas

The most basic sentence structures are simple sentences. They are single clauses that make sense on their own, containing one subject and one verb. For example, 'Kathy H is an unreliable narrator.' or 'The First World War began in 1914.'

Academic writing should not contain many of these sentences because, as their name suggests, they seem simple. However, they are an excellent way to establish ideas at the start of paragraphs and to emphasise part of your conclusion at the end of an essay.

Link important information

A compound sentence is two clauses joined by a conjunction. Both clauses should make sense on their own. For example, 'Ruth dominates Kathy but this often reveals Ruth's own insecurities.' Again, you should avoid writing lots of compound sentences but they can be useful to specifically link together key concepts that you have discovered or that you plan to explore.

Develop your points

Most of your writing should be in the form of complex sentences as the subordinate clause allows you to develop your comments in greater detail. For example:

> Kathy H can be viewed as an unreliable narrator, sometimes admitting that she may be 'remembering it wrong' during her narrative.

Remember to vary where you place your subordinate clauses (before, after or in the middle of your main clauses) to stop your writing becoming repetitive.

Highlight key findings

A number of structural devices can be used to emphasise important information in your exam answers. However, they must be used sparingly to ensure they have impact.

Lists and patterns of three are useful ways to present facts, examples, evidence or different aspects of your argument. For example:

> A fraudulent election result, being a rich landowner and his discrimination against Buddhists made Diem an unpopular leader in South Vietnam.

Antithesis, the juxtaposition of opposite ideas, can be used to highlight the contrasting aspects of a single concept. For example, 'Urban change has created cultural diversity but also cultural divisions.'

Parallelism emphasises ideas by arranging them in a repeated grammatical structure. The same determiner, word class, pronoun, tense, etc. is placed in the same position in subsequent clauses. For example:

> No aid, no investment and no debt relief means the development gap will widen.

> There are many benefits of transnational companies: they create jobs, they offer education, they strengthen communities and they improve infrastructure.

Summary

- Use simple sentences to establish ideas.
- Use compound sentences to link ideas.
- Use complex sentences to develop ideas (but vary the position of your subordinate clauses).
- Highlight key information through lists, patterns of three, antithesis and parallelism.

Sample paragraph

The paragraph below is a response to an English Language exam question. Notice the simple sentence to establish the point, the compound sentence to link ideas together, the complex sentences (with the subordinate clauses in different positions) to develop the student's analysis, and the antithesis to highlight a key idea about the text.

> The setting has a disturbing atmosphere. The room is attractive but it also appears to have a terrible past. Using colours that are traditionally associated with happiness, the writer's description of 'pinks and yellows blossoming across the floral wallpaper' initially creates a pleasant impression. This is emphasised by the 'blossoming' metaphor, making the setting seem vibrant and almost alive. However, through the use of contrasting images, the writer presents the room as a place of death rather than a place of life. The wallpaper is 'flecked with bloodstains' and 'torn away as if in terror', implying some unspecified horrific event.

Questions

QUICK TEST
1. How many verbs should appear in a simple sentence?
2. What should be used to link the clauses in a compound sentence?
3. Turn the two sentences below into one complex sentence.
    Stevenson describes Mr Utterson as reading a book of 'some dry divinity' before going 'soberly and gratefully to bed'. This quotation uses a reference to religion and the adverb 'soberly' to suggest that he lives a respectable life.

PRACTISE USING SENTENCE STRUCTURES TO ENHANCE YOUR MEANING
Look back at one of your previous exam answers. Can you improve the sophistication of your response by using different sentence structures for specific purposes?

Improve Your Skills

Be Sophisticated

Improve 1

1. Read the two sample paragraphs below. Both show an understanding of Charles Dickens's novel *Great Expectations* and the exam question's assessment objectives. However, the second version is written more effectively. List what has been done to make the second version more sophisticated.

   Dickens shows that Miss Haversham is quite weird and this is especially true when he compares her to one of Pip's memories. 'A skeleton in the ashes of a rich dress.' I think this shows the reader different aspects of her character because she is a figure of fear and she also demands sympathy with the image of the skeleton having a fearful tone while also showing she is like the walking dead. The melancholy depiction of the 'rich' dress in 'ashes' means that she was once wealthy but has lost her beauty and status. I think some of Pip's fear is also due to the characters' vastly different social positions.

   Miss Havisham is presented as disconcerting by Dickens. Comparing her to Pip's memory of 'a skeleton in the ashes of a rich dress' confronts the reader with conflicting aspects of her character. She is a figure of fear but she also demands sympathy. The image of the skeleton has a sinister tone while simultaneously conveying how she lacks life, happiness and hope. Some of Pip's unease is due to the characters' vastly different social positions, perhaps being implied through the reference to the 'rich' dress. However, the melancholy depiction of it in 'ashes' could symbolise Miss Haversham's loss of beauty and status.

2. Read the sentences of poetry analysis below. Rephrase each one to make it more formal.

   a. Sheers uses a soppy simile to show they're touching each other.

   b. Hardy gives us a couple who are physically close but streets apart in how they feel about each other.

   c. The bit that says 'half broken-hearted' suggests just how glum he's feeling right now.

3. Rewrite the following paragraph to give the vocabulary a more academic style.

   Economic change may provide one explanation for the decline in tying the knot. Due to house prices going through the roof, young adults don't stray from the nest cos they need to save up for a mortgage. People would rather start climbing the housing ladder than get married because having bricks and mortar is more important than a piece of paper. And don't get me started on the sky-rocketing costs of an old-fashioned white wedding, heightened by all your mates begging you to have a massive party blowout. And men especially might be less likely to want a wedding because living with parents seems lame for a lad so what I mean is, when push comes to shove, when you have to choose between a wedding and a house deposit they're just going to shack up together.

Improve 2

4. Identify whether the following sentences are simple, compound or complex.
   a. Transferring energy through wires as electricity, electrons have a negative charge.
   b. A fuse is one component that can be found in an electrical circuit.
   c. Electric current is measured in amps while the charge is measured in coulombs.
   d. Total resistance, due to the current being able to follow multiple paths, is reduced in parallel circuits.
5. Rewrite the sentences below with correct use of full stops and capital letters.
   a. Fossils have been discovered all over the planet they allow scientists to explore the extent to which organisms on earth have evolved.
   b. One example of an erosional feature found on a headland is durdle door this is a limestone arch in dorset, probably caused by hydraulic action and abrasion.
   c. Edward the confessor died in january 1066 william of normandy claimed that he was the rightful heir and invaded england however, harold godwinson and harald hardrada also believed they had a claim to the throne.
6. Look at the sentences below and identify where they need apostrophes.
   a. The laws effectiveness has been questioned by recent historians.
   b. This areas high risk of erosion could mean that managed retreat is one of the councils options.
   c. Darwins theory of evolution was pre-dated by Lamarcks theories.

7. Rewrite the complex sentences below, adding in the correct commas.
   a. Despite her innocence Juliet is also presented as impulsive.
   b. Lord Capulet is initially presented as aggressive demanding his sword so he can join in the fight against the Montagues.
   c. Shakespeare presents Mercutio despite his coarse sense of humour as a tragic victim of the families' conflict.

8. Correct the punctuation in the following sentences.
   a. Despite his almost comical appearance it becomes clear that Piggy is the most intelligent and rational of the main characters.
   b. Simon is presented as morally and spiritually good contrasting with the savagery that emerges in the other boys.
   c. Ralph who is quickly elected as leader by the marooned schoolboys is charismatic and dynamic.

Improve 3

9. Rewrite the complex sentences below, each time moving the subordinate clause into an alternative position.
   a. Having fought valiantly in battle, Macbeth is made Thane of Cawdor by King Duncan.
   b. Lady Macbeth is presented as manipulative, quickly tempting her husband to fulfil his ambitions.
   c. Malcolm, despite being an honest and innocent man, initially presents himself to Macduff as immoral and tyrannical.

10. Rewrite the following answers, integrating the evidence into a single sentence.
    a. Macbeth's repetition of the witches' language from Act 1 scene 1 foreshadows how they will come to influence his fate. This can be seen in the line, 'So foul and fair a day I have not seen'.
    b. Secondary microplastics are having a serious impact on marine ecosystems. These come from sources like water bottles, fishing nets and plastic bags.

11. Turn the following three sentences into one complex sentence.

    Jack uses insulting and imperative language. 'Shut up, Fatty'. This conveys his cruel attitude towards Piggy and his sense of superiority.

12. Rewrite the following paragraph so it is in the third person.

    In my opinion, weather in the UK is becoming more extreme. My research showed that, in the last thirty years, there has been more heavy rain and floods, heavy snowfall, and heatwaves and drought. I believe that climate change may be the cause of this increase in the frequency and intensity of extreme weather.

13. Rewrite the following paragraph to show more caution in the interpretations being made.

    Dharker's poem 'Tissue' is about the need to share the world rather than rule it. The lines 'The sun shines through / their borderlines, the marks / that rivers make, roads' refer to features of maps because they convey how humans divide themselves rather than living in harmony. Using the image of sunlight and transparency means that Dharker hopes love and humanity will help people see beyond such divisions.

Modelled GCSE Answer: English Language

In the Exam

This double page provides an annotated version of a GCSE English Language response that displays a good level of academic writing.

> He was one of those reckless, rattlepated, openhearted, and open-mouthed young gentlemen who possess the gift of familiarity in its highest perfection, and who scramble carelessly along the journey of life, making friends, as the phrase is, wherever they go. His father was a rich manufacturer, and had bought landed property enough in one of the midland counties to make all the born squires in his neighbourhood thoroughly envious of him. Arthur was his only son, possessor in prospect of the great estate and the great business after his father's death; well supplied with money, and not too rigidly looked after, during his father's lifetime. Report, or scandal, whichever you please, said that the old gentleman had been rather wild in his youthful days, and that, unlike most parents, he was not disposed to be violently indignant when he found that his son took after him. This may be true or not. I myself only knew the elder Mr. Holliday when he was getting on in years, and then he was as quiet and as respectable a gentleman as ever I met with.
>
> (from *The Dead Hand* by Wilkie Collins)

How does the writer use language to present the character of Arthur? **[8 marks]**

A list of adjectives, 'reckless, rattlepated, openhearted, and open-mouthed', is used by the writer (1) to present Arthur as wild but good-natured (2). The first two words appear critical, suggesting that he does not think about his actions. The list gives the sentence a fast pace, perhaps reflecting the way in which Arthur lives his life (3), and this is later emphasised by the verb 'scramble'. However (4), a sense of kindness and childlike curiosity is also portrayed through the words 'openhearted, and open-mouthed', and this is reinforced at the end of the sentence by the reference to him 'making friends' wherever he goes (5).

Arthur's wildness is linked to him being from a rich family (6), possibly indicating that he does not have to work for a living. Writing that Arthur will inherit 'the great estate and the great business', the author uses repetition to highlight the idea of wealth. This (7) is developed by the comment that Arthur has always been 'well supplied with money', which could additionally imply that he does not understand the hardships of an average life.

The author also links Arthur's profligate behaviour to his upbringing (8). When it is stated that he has not been 'rigidly looked after', the adverb conveys a lack of discipline. This phrase could also be interpreted as a lack of love, although the reference to him being the 'only son' appears to be suggesting that he was spoiled (9). Adding (10) that Arthur's father had also been linked to 'scandal' reinforces the notion that he may not have received enough moral guidance as a child.

Some of the following features of academic writing appear more than once in the answer.
1. The passive voice focuses the answer on features of language.
2. The answer is focused clearly on the question. It is written in the third person, subject-specific language has been used and the quotations have been embedded.
3. Cautious language when developing the interpretation.
4. Development phrases are used within paragraphs to keep track of the different ideas being explored.
5. Vocabulary choices are varied, precise, formal and succinct.
6. Topic statement, clearly linked to the question, to establish a new point in a new paragraph.
7. A demonstrative link to develop analysis.
8. A simple sentence to establish a new point, followed by a complex sentence to develop the analysis. Sentences throughout the answer are punctuated accurately and subordinate clauses have been placed in different positions in complex sentences.
9. Alternative interpretation, emphasised by the use of the compound sentence.
10. Varied sentence openers have been used throughout the answer.

In the Exam

Modelled GCSE Answer: English Literature

This double page provides an annotated version of a GCSE English Literature response that displays a good level of academic writing.

How does Priestley use the Birlings to explore ideas about respectability in *An Inspector Calls*? [30 marks]

The characters of the Birlings are used by Priestley to explore the idea that respectability can be a façade. Despite their apparent middle-class respectability, each character's moral corruption is gradually revealed by the Inspector (1).

The initial presentation of Mr and Mrs Birling is as upright members of their community (2). Mr Birling points out that he 'was Lord Mayor … there's a very good chance of a knighthood' and Mrs Birling talks '[with dignity]' about her 'great deal of useful work' for charity (3). References to status imply that Mr Birling has a good reputation and has been entrusted with positions of responsibility while the adjectives (4) 'great' and 'useful' suggest his wife's similar social standing. The pre-war class system often brought automatic status to wealthier people but there is a clear implication that the Birlings have also worked to improve their community alongside their standing within that community (5). This status (6) is reflected in the manner in which they speak, with the stage direction for Mrs Birling conveying (7) her awareness of their high position.

However (8), the selfishness and hubris of the Birling parents is exposed by Priestley in order to make the audience question their outward respectability. Mr Birling's comment about his sacking of Eva Smith, 'if you don't come down sharply on some of these people', shows that he made an example of her in order to suppress further strike action. The adverb 'sharply' suggests an awareness that he treated her unfairly, but indicates a lack of concern (9). Worse is the attitude implied by his use of the phrase 'these people': the working classes are a different, lesser breed (10). Birling's actions are not respectable; his actions are callous and dishonourable (11).

Mrs Birling is similarly derisive of people below her own social class (12). Although she presents herself as charitable, linking to the Christian virtues expected of respectable citizens at the time, she dismisses Eva as 'a girl of that sort' because she is unmarried. Instead of compassion, the use of the determiner 'that' suggests a dislike of others less privileged. Eva's own attempts at displaying respect are condemned as 'ridiculous airs' while Mrs Birling admits to disliking her and therefore having 'used my influence' to stop the girl receiving any charity. The abstract noun 'influence' shows her corruption as she misuses the power that comes with her façade of respectability in order to hurt another person (13).

This pretence of respectability is also explored through the Birlings' children. Sheila is preparing to marry into the distinguished Croft family while Eric has been public schooled, university educated and has a position of trust in the Birling family business (14). Regarding the sacking of Eva, the Inspector's evaluation of how Sheila decided to 'punish the girl just because she made you feel like that' exposes her character as rude, jealous and vindictive (15). The verb 'punish' shows an abuse of power similar to her parents' while the adverb 'just' highlights how her actions were extreme and thoughtless. Moreover, Eric is a secret alcoholic and it is implied that he raped Eva Smith (16). His words, 'I was in that state when a chap easily turns nasty … I didn't even remember – that's the hellish thing', could suggest regret but the tone appears to be more self-pitying (17).

42 In the Exam

The adverb 'easily' might be seen as seeking to reduce his responsibility while the use of the first-person pronoun keeps the focus on his emotional experience rather than that of his victim. However, the Inspector asserts that Eric 'used her … as if she was an animal, a thing, not a person', employing the pattern of three to emphasise his contemptible behaviour (18).

Throughout the play, the Birlings are shown to project an image of respectability that appears to be partly assumed simply because of their social class. However, Priestley routinely exposes this as a façade through the characters' actions and intentions (19). Even towards the end of the play, Mr Birling's main priority is 'to cover this up as soon as I can' rather than to learn from the experience and try to live a more genuinely respectable life.

Some of the following features of academic writing appear more than once in the essay.

1. Clear focus on the question, written in the third person and using the passive voice.
2. Clear topic sentence, making use of nominalisation at the start.
3. Use of embedded evidence.
4. Subject- and topic-specific vocabulary. Writing is appropriately formal.
5. The context has been integrated within the analysis, rather than being tagged onto the end of the paragraph.
6. Demonstrative link to emphasise that the essay is being kept on track.
7. Synonyms used to avoid the repetition of show (present, imply, suggest, reflect, convey) and respectable (upright, reputation, social standing, entrusted).
8. Development link to start the new paragraph.
9. Varied vocabulary is being used with a good degree of precision and a range of complex sentences are punctuated accurately.
10. Use of a colon for elaboration.
11. Antithesis to emphasise a key comment.
12. Simple sentence to establish a point.
13. This paragraph is typical of the succinctness used throughout the essay, avoiding synonym pairs, unnecessary intensifiers, figurative language, etc.
14. Noun phrases have been used to keep this information succinct.
15. Pattern of three to emphasise why Sheila's behaviour is not respectable.
16. Use of caution in the interpretation.
17. Acknowledgement of alternative interpretation.
18. Vocabulary choices use shades of meaning in order to convey different levels of criticism for Sheila's and Eric's behaviour.
19. Similar language to the introduction to emphasise the notion of a conclusion.

In the Exam: Improve Two GCSE Answers: English Language and English Literature

Read the two exam responses, then consider how the student's work could be more concise, precise and sophisticated. Using your academic writing skills, rewrite both responses.

English Language

How does the writer use language to present the character of Countess Narona?

[8 marks]

> The accent was foreign; the tone was low and firm. Her fingers closed gently, and yet resolutely, on the Doctor's arm. Neither her language nor her action had the slightest effect in inclining him to grant her request. The influence that instantly stopped him, on the way to his carriage, was the silent influence of her face. The startling contrast between the corpse-like pallor of her complexion and the overpowering life and light, the glittering metallic brightness in her large black eyes, held him spell-bound. She was dressed in dark colours, with perfect taste; she was of middle height, and (apparently) of middle age—say a year or two over thirty. Her lower features—the nose, mouth, and chin—possessed the fineness and delicacy of form which is oftener seen among women of foreign races than among women of English birth. She was unquestionably a handsome person—with the one serious drawback of her ghastly complexion, and with the less noticeable defect of a total want of tenderness in the expression of her eyes. Apart from his first emotion of surprise, the feeling she produced in the Doctor may be described as an overpowering feeling of professional curiosity.
>
> (from *The Haunted Hotel* by Wilkie Collins)

The Countess is presented as looking really ill. The author describes her 'corpse-like pallor … her ghastly complexion'. He uses the words to make her sound as good as dead. Her illness also makes her look frightening and scary. The 'dark colours' of her clothing mean that she is unhappy as if all the light in the world has gone out in her soul. The Countess is also presented as looking unusual. The author describes how her complexion is a stark contrast to her eyes. 'the overpowering life and light, the glittering metallic brightness.' Her eyes look different to her face. The author uses the words 'life', 'light' and 'brightness' to make her sound beautiful and full of energy. This is emphasised by the words 'glittering' and 'overpowering', making her sound really hot and sexy. The author also says her eyes have 'a total want of tenderness', making her sound hard and emotionless despite her beauty. The Countess's beauty is developed when the author describes how it 'held him spellbound' and this metaphor makes her attractiveness sound like a spell and her 'fineness and delicacy of form' makes her sound pretty. The author also describes her as 'foreign' which means that her beauty also comes from her being exotic.

English Literature

Explore how Shakespeare presents Lady Macbeth as a controlling character. [30 marks]

In the first half of the play *Macbeth*, Shakespeare presents Lady Macbeth as a controlling character by showing different ways in which she controls people and situations.

In Act 1 scenes 5 and 7, Shakespeare presents Lady Macbeth as controlling by presenting her as tempting Macbeth to kill the king. 'Give solely sovereign sway and masterdom.' This shows that Macbeth will gain sway and masterdom if he becomes king. The use of the word 'solely' shows that he will have more power than anyone else. Shakespeare also presents Lady Macbeth as tempting Macbeth to kill the king when she totally convinces him that they'll get away with the murder. 'we'll not fail … his spongy officers, who shall bear the guilt.' The word 'guilt' is important and she tries to make him more confident by telling him he'll feel okay. Lady Macbeth understands Macbeth's fears of going against the divine right of kings and ending up in Hell so she tries to make him more confident.

Shakespeare presents Macbeth as easily bullied, like a child. He doesn't like it when Lady Macbeth says, 'What beast was't then, / That made you break this enterprise to me? / When you durst do it, then you were a man', in these lines he doesn't like her calling him a coward as the word 'durst' is in the past tense which means he isn't brave anymore. The way she questions him is a key feature of her controlling character and the word 'beast' is supposed to sound sarcastic. This would make Macbeth feel humiliated. He wouldn't like being called a coward because men were more important than women and he has always been known as a brave soldier.

Shakespeare presents Lady Macbeth as controlling because she gives orders and imperatives to Macbeth. 'go, carry them, and smear / The sleepy grooms with blood.' This has three orders in one speech making her sound very controlling. It would be unusual for women at the time to be in control of their husbands so this makes Lady Macbeth seem more controlling than normal.

In Act 2 scene 2, some of Lady Macbeth's orders are to control Macbeth in a good way. She says, 'Consider it not so deeply.' She uses the word 'deeply' to show that she worries about Macbeth's state of mind and wants him not to worry as it could ruin everything. She is aware that he is worried about having broken the Great Chain of Being.

Shakespeare also presents Lady Macbeth as controlling different situations. In Act 1 scene 5, she says the bit about, 'bear welcome in your eye, / Your hand, your tongue: look like th'innocent flower'. This is a metaphor and a simile. It shows that she can pretend to be nice and wants to teach Macbeth to be able to control situations like she can. She shows this side of her character in Act 1 scene 6 when she speaks to the King. 'All our service, / In every point twice done, and then double done.' She uses the word 'service' to pretend she respects him. She also pretends she respects him by repeating the word 'done' to mean she will do anything for him.

Later on, Shakespeare shows Lady Macbeth trying to control the whole of the banquet to save Macbeth's face. She jokes Macbeth into submission by comparing him to a woman and calling the ghost 'the very painting of your fear'. This is another metaphor and it means the ghost doesn't exist so he should stop acting like such a weirdo. Throughout the play, Shakespeare presents her trying to control others to gain more power. She succeeds in manipulating Macbeth into killing the King but she can't really control his thoughts and feelings after the killing.

Improve Two GCSE Answers: English Language and English Literature

Answers

Pages 4–5
1. The first half is focused and analytical. However, the second half focuses incorrectly on the man's job rather than his family and doesn't include analysis (the 'how' part of the question) or comparison.
2. The house has a swimming pool in the basement ~~which is a really relaxing place to swim~~; the master bedroom ~~is lovely as it~~ has an en suite; the house was originally built in 1888; it is detached ~~which makes it feel quieter and more private~~. (The question asked for facts; the deleted extra details are descriptive opinions.)

Pages 6–7
1. During ~~the scientific process of~~ photosynthesis, plants transform energy from the Sun ~~and this light energy is then converted~~ into chemical energy ~~that the plants need~~.
2. Volcanoes occur when magma rises ~~right~~ to the Earth's surface, creating gas bubbles of ~~really~~ high pressure that eventually explode.
3. Sample answer: Lady Macbeth's guilt develops into madness.
4. The ~~poor people and~~ peasants started to revolt in 1381 due to anger ~~and fury~~ at their lack of freedom and equality~~, and the restrictions placed upon them~~.

Pages 8–9
1. acceptance   2. forgiveness
3. Mount Pinatubo's volcanic eruption in 1991 …
4. The Labour Party's founding of the NHS in 1948 provided free healthcare for all citizens in the United Kingdom.

Pages 10–13
1. Stevenson's animalistic descriptions of Mr Hyde (a), such as 'apelike fury' and 'masked thing like a monkey', draw on Darwin's theory of evolution (b). The implication that Hyde has devolved (c), becoming the opposite (d) of a Victorian gentleman, is (e) emphasised by the contrast between 'fury' and the reader's expectations of civilised behaviour. (f) A sense of disgust (g) is (h) conveyed by the noun 'thing', suggesting that Poole (i) can hardly bring himself to describe Hyde.
   a. Nominalisation
   b. The sentence has been cut short to keep the paragraph focused on Hyde rather than Darwin. The tagged-on feature-spotting has also been deleted.
   c. Nominalisation.
   d. Metaphor has been replaced with plain English.
   e. The unnecessary intensifier has been removed.
   f. The next sentence has been cut to keep the focus on Hyde rather than the character of Utterson.
   g. The unnecessary synonym has been removed.
   h. The unnecessary intensifier has been removed.
   i. The storytelling in parenthesis has been removed to keep the paragraph focused on analysis.
2. a. i; b. iii; c. iii
3. The answer contains an explanation of what tropical storms are and where they occur, rather than focusing on why climate change may cause their wider distribution. The first two sentences and the last one are not needed.
4. The author begins the story by focusing the reader on the sinister ~~and creepy~~ atmosphere. By describing 'the heavy darkness' and the 'constantly shifting shadows', the author ~~totally~~ unnerves the reader and creates a sense of danger ~~that is like a warning bell for us~~. ~~This creates an ominous tone which reminds me of an episode of 'Stranger Things'~~. This ominous tone may be effective in engaging the audience as ~~it grabs the audience's attention and~~ it would make them ~~really~~ consider what will happen when characters ~~and people~~ are introduced to the scene.
5. A variety of prosaic words or phrases could be used, e.g.
   a. volatile, lacked stability
   b. contain a variety, are home to a number
   c. becomes angry, loses his temper
   d. increased, expanded
   e. becomes a tyrant, starts to behave inhumanely
6. a. Priestley's 1940's play …
   b. The seeds experiment …
   c. Java's many active volcanoes …
7. conclusion, creation, decision, development, exploration, interpretation, introduction, production, success (or succession), summary
8. a. In conclusion, plants …
   b. Shakespeare's development of Benvolio displays …
   c. Golding's introduction of Jack …
9. a. Sheila's remorse at the end of the play leads …
   b. The government's introduction of the 1916 Military Service Act imposed conscription on all single men between 18 and 41, providing the United Kingdom …
10. Your rewritten paragraph might read similarly to this: The presentation of Lord Capulet in Act 3 scene 5 as authoritarian and cruel, when he gives Juliet the ultimatum to marry Paris or 'hang! Beg! Starve! Die in the streets! / For by my soul I'll ne'er acknowledge thee', is very different from the loving father of Act 1 scene 2. Shakespeare's list of verbs conveys Capulet's cruelty but also his awareness of the economic power he has over his daughter: she has been brought up to rely on a father or husband, rather than to be able to support herself. The exclamation marks suggest the words should be shouted, increasing the audience's sense of his power. Capulet's threat to cut Juliet off from the family emphasises his harshness, revealing that his previous unconditional love for her is dependent upon her following his orders.

Pages 14–15
1. love   2. honourable   3. shocking   4. avaricious

Pages 16–17
1. Subject-specific words appear throughout a course; topic-specific words feature in individual units or exam questions.
2. a. simile   b. metaphor   c. symbolism   d. repetition
   e. character

Pages 18–19
1. this, that, these, those
2. a. Sequence   b. Addition   c. Contrast
   d. Cause and effect   e. Comparison

Pages 20–21
1. It must make sense on its own / be a main clause.
2. After 'multiple ways'.
3. 'In other words'; 'In essence'
4. To show that, while you have a clear viewpoint, you can see the validity of other perspectives.

Pages 22–25
1. Whereas (a) she is calm and manipulative (b) earlier in the play, by Act 5 scene 1 Lady Macbeth is presented as being stricken by madness (c). This is conveyed (d) through deliberately disconnected sentences such as, 'Out, damned spot! out, I say! – One: two: why, then, 'tis time to do't. – Hell is murky!', which show none of her previous skills of rhetoric (e): she now seems barely coherent (f). The regular pauses and exclamation marks (g) indicate that her speech should be performed in a distracted yet urgent tone (h). In other words, she appears out of control rather than controlling (i). The references to the murder of the King (the 'spot' of blood and 'time to do't') suggest that this (j) madness has been caused by her guilt (k), contrasting with (l) her unconcerned attitude in Act 2 scene 2. Alternatively (m), as regicide (n) was seen as a crime against God, the adjective (o) 'damned' and the comment that 'Hell is murky' could imply that it is a fear of eternal punishment that has caused this (p) insanity.
   a. Discourse marker to show development of the essay.
   b. Topic-specific language.
   c. Topic sentence to establish a new point.
   d. Subject-specific language.
   e. Subject-specific language.
   f. Use of colon for elaboration.
   g. A range of subject-specific language.
   h. Precise use of language showing shades of meaning.
   i. Restating to clarify a key point.
   j. Demonstrative link.
   k. Topic-specific language.
   l. Discourse marker to make a development link.
   m. Use of alternative perspective.
   n. Topic-specific language.
   o. Subject-specific language.
   p. Demonstrative link.
2. a. verbs b. adjectives c. simile d. metaphor
   e. personification
3. a. Your own subject- and topic-specific words.
   b. Your own paragraph.
4. More precise alternatives include:
   a. serious, major   b. damage, hurt
   c. liked, enjoyed   d. tired, exhausted
5. Suggested answers:
   a. satisfied, pleased, merry, delighted, jubilant
   b. sorry, downcast, unhappy, miserable, heartbroken
   c. uncertain, risky, threatening, treacherous, deadly
6. a. strange, creepy, sinister, frightening, terrifying
   b. Answers might include: (low intensity) spooky, weird, unnerving; (average) eerie, disturbing, ominous, threatening; (high) chilling, petrifying, alarming.
   c. Answers should show clear shades of meaning. For example: A creepy setting is established through the author's use of simile. Describing the wind as being 'like a whisper' creates an unnerving mood. The setting is made more disturbing by the description of the shadows, with the verb 'flitted' suggesting that something threatening is trying to stay hidden. The final sentence increases the feeling of horror. This is achieved by the use of the adverb 'suddenly' and the metaphor 'ripped through the night' to shock the reader. The adjective 'blood-curdling', along with the abstract nouns 'shock' and 'pain', evoke a feeling of terror.
   d. Your own synonyms.
7. b
8. a. Shakespeare's plays can be sorted into three different genres: comedy, tragedy and history.
   Sample answer: The periodic table is structured to show periodic trends of the chemical elements: they are arranged by atomic number, electron configuration and recurring properties.
   b. In other words, plants are vital for the oxygen content of the Earth's atmosphere. or In other words, plants need light, water and carbon dioxide to survive.
9. Sample answer (topic sentence, demonstratives links and development links are underlined):
   'Exposure' and 'The Charge of the Light Brigade' both present the horrors of war. Owen focuses on the brutal conditions: 'the merciless iced east winds that knive us', using personification to suggest that the men feel under attack by the weather. This sense of attack is highlighted by the use of the verb 'knive' to convey the soldiers' physical pain, and the way the adjective 'merciless' suggests there is no respite. In comparison, Tennyson focuses more on the fighting. His use of anaphora in 'Cannon to right of them, / Cannon to left of them, / Cannon behind them' creates a similar image of soldiers being under constant attack. The use of the prepositions emphasises this impression that there is no escape.

Pages 26–27
1. Reigning from 1558 to 1603, one of Elizabeth I's …
2. Despite threats from Catholics and Puritans, Elizabeth …
3. Often called the 'golden age' of culture, Elizabeth's …
4. Both clauses are main clauses so the comma should be a full stop or a conjunction such as 'and'. Or the sentence could be rewritten so the second clause is subordinate: Tensions grew between Spain and England, culminating …

Pages 28–29
1. Sample answer: The first paragraph shows how cold the boy is, with verbs like 'shivering' conveying his reaction to the low temperature. This is reinforced in the description of the setting, with the use of nouns such as 'icicle' and 'snow' to suggest that it is freezing.
2. Sample answer: When Heaney describes his father and the horse as a 'sweating team … his eye narrowed and angled at the ground', he could be suggesting that he was impressed by how hard his father worked.

Pages 30–31
1. Personal
2. Shakespeare presents Macbeth as a tragically flawed individual.
3. In the active voice, the subject of the sentence does something to the object (it focuses on actions). In the passive voice, the subject of the sentence has something done to it by the object (it focuses more on results).
4. Mrs Birling is presented as a hypocrite by Priestley.

Pages 32–33
1. Sample answer: The Battle of Stamford Bridge, which ended in the killing of Godwinson, Hardrada and the majority of the Norwegian forces, was a decisive victory for King Harold.
2. Sample answer: Various strategies, such as water and soil management, tree planting and appropriate use of technology, can be used to reduce the risk of desertification.

Pages 34–35

1. One   2. A conjunction (and, but, or, so, etc.)
3. Stevenson describes Mr Utterson as reading a book of 'some dry divinity' before going 'soberly and gratefully to bed', using a reference to religion and the adverb 'soberly' to suggest that he lives a respectable life.

Pages 36–39

1. Miss Havisham is presented as disconcerting by Dickens (a). Comparing her to Pip's memory of 'a skeleton in the ashes of a rich dress' (b), the reader is confronted with conflicting aspects of her character (c). She is a figure of fear but she also demands sympathy (d). The image of the skeleton has a sinister tone while simultaneously conveying how she lacks life, happiness and hope (e). Some of Pip's unease is due to the characters' vastly different social positions, perhaps being implied through the reference to the 'rich' dress (f). However, the melancholy depiction of it in 'ashes' could symbolise Miss Haversham's loss of beauty and status (g).
    a. The opening has been restricted to a simple sentence to establish the point more clearly. The language is more formal and is in the passive voice.
    b. The quotation has been embedded.
    c. Language is more varied (avoiding repetition of 'show'); a complex sentence has been used to show development; the sentence is in the third person.
    d. A compound sentence has been used to link two ideas; this is more effective than the long, poorly punctuated sentence in the first version.
    e. The language is more varied (avoiding repetition of 'fear' and 'also'). A pattern of three is used to emphasise a key idea and replaces the informal reference to 'the walking dead'.
    f. The context sentence is embedded within the analysis rather than tagged on the end of the paragraph. The first person has been removed and the sentence openings are more varied. A complex sentence has been used to show development. Cautious language ('perhaps') has been used for the interpretation of what the dress may symbolise.
    g. Caution is used again.
2. More formal phrasing may include:
    a. Sheers uses a romantic simile to convey intimacy.
    b. Hardy presents a couple who are physically close but emotionally distant.
    c. The metaphor 'half broken-hearted' suggests the depth of his unhappiness.
3. Sample answer: Economic change may provide one explanation for the decline in marriage. Due to the rising cost of housing, young adults stay living with their parents longer in order to save up for a mortgage. Furthermore, people would rather buy a house because material security is more important than the security of marriage. This also links to the rising costs of a traditional wedding, heightened by additional social expectations of a big celebration. In addition, men especially might be less likely to marry because living with parents is not perceived as masculine, so the choice between spending money on a wedding or on a house deposit may lead people to simply co-habit.
4. a. Complex   b. Simple   c. Compound   d. Complex
5. a. Fossils have been discovered all over the planet. They allow scientists to explore the extent to which organisms on Earth have evolved.
    b. One example of an erosional feature found on a headland is Durdle Door. This is a limestone arch in Dorset, probably caused by hydraulic action and abrasion.
    c. Edward the Confessor died in January 1066. William of Normandy claimed that he was the rightful heir and invaded England. However, Harold Godwinson and Harald Hardrada also believed they had a claim to the throne.
6. a. The **law's** effectiveness…
    b. This **area's** high risk … **council's** options.
    c. **Darwin's** theory … **Lamarck's** theories.
7. a. Despite her innocence, Juliet is …
    b. Lord Capulet is initially presented as aggressive, demanding …
    c. Shakespeare presents Mercutio, despite his coarse sense of humour, as a tragic victim …
8. a. Despite his almost comical appearance, it becomes clear that Piggy is the most intelligent and rational of the main characters.
    b. Simon is presented as morally and spiritually good, contrasting with the savagery that emerges in the other boys.
    c. Ralph, who is quickly elected as leader by the marooned schoolboys, is charismatic and dynamic.
9. a. Macbeth, having fought valiantly in battle, is made Thane of Cawdor by King Duncan.
    Macbeth is made Thane of Cawdor by King Duncan, having fought valiantly in battle.
    b. Quickly tempting her husband to fulfil his ambitions, Lady Macbeth is presented as manipulative.
    Lady Macbeth, quickly tempting her husband to fulfil his ambitions, is presented as manipulative.
    c. Despite being an honest and innocent man, Malcolm initially presents himself to Macduff as immoral and tyrannical.
    Malcolm initially presents himself to Macduff as immoral and tyrannical, despite being an honest and innocent man.
10. a. Macbeth's repetition of the witches' language from Act 1 scene 1, 'So foul and fair a day I have not seen', foreshadows how they will come to influence his fate.
    b. Secondary microplastics, from sources like water bottles, fishing nets and plastic bags, are having a serious impact on marine ecosystems.
11. Jack uses insulting and imperative language, 'Shut up, Fatty', conveying his cruel attitude towards Piggy and his sense of superiority.
12. Weather in the UK is becoming more extreme. Research shows that, in the last thirty years, there has been more heavy rain and floods, heavy snowfall, and heatwaves and drought. Climate change may be the cause of this increase in the frequency and intensity of extreme weather.
13. Sample answer: Dharker's poem 'Tissue' suggests the need to share the world rather than rule it. The lines 'The sun shines through / their borderlines, the marks / that rivers make, roads' refer to features of maps to perhaps convey how humans divide themselves rather than living in harmony. Using the image of sunlight and transparency could depict Dharker's hope that love and humanity will help people see beyond such divisions.